God Gives Second Chances

A Tiny Testimonial from the Heart

Jeanine M. Jones

Jeanine M. Jones
P.O. Box 56
Washington, MI 48094
www.jeaninemjonesauthor.com

God Gives Second Chances: A Tiny Testimonial from the Heart / Jeanine M. Jones, 1st Edition

ISBN 979-8-9946172-0-5

Edited and formatted by Katie Erickson, KatieEricksonEditing.com
Author photograph courtesy of Glenn Cruickshank Photography

In honor of my parents,
who were loving examples of a life well lived.

Preface

When it comes to matters of the heart, I don't mess around. I'm not referring to our emotions, although emotions definitely play a part in this story. No, I'm speaking of our physical hearts – flesh and blood, life and death.

All choices and decisions in life come with consequences, either good or bad. This story is one where choices were made with the best of intentions, but they resulted in unforeseen consequences. Negative results or dire circumstances may be assumed, and that is partially correct. But more than anything, these unforeseen consequences were far from negative.

This is my testimony of the heart, which took place many years ago, but is still as meaningful now as when it actually happened. It is a story that is universal in theme. It is a story of a desire to do what is right, losing focus and purpose along the way, and a journey back to redemption through our loving God. My choices and decisions did result in a season of anxiety and fear, but also in awe and reverence of the God I worship and adore.

Acknowledgments

As an author new to the entire world of writing, I've had an eventful, if rather circuitous, journey to date, beginning as the owner and writer of two mental health blogs, *The Heart's Way, Imagery and Insights,* and *The Heart's Way for Creative Clinicians.* The blogs faltered after several years of effort due to my inability to keep up with the stress of creating content weekly, along with full-time employment.

Not wanting to "give up," I transitioned to writing a book, which was planned to be a "one and done" project. That book is still not quite finished, but hopefully it will be published in the near future. In the meantime, I have learned so much about writing and self-publishing. The advice? Start "small," in order to figure things out. So, friends, you are reading a very short work. In fact, it is called a tiny testimonial. We have to start somewhere, right?

Even for such a small book, many people have been supportive. I'd like to take a moment to acknowledge them.

First and foremost, I would not be writing this – or writing anything in fact – without the guidance, love, and grace of God. Lord, thank You for whispering gently behind me to follow Your path. I would be nothing without You.

"Whether you turn to the right or to the left, your ears will hear a voice behind you, saying, 'This is the way; walk in it.'"
(Isaiah 30:21 NIV)

When nudged to begin writing a book, I came upon some sage advice by CJ and Shelley Hitz at Christian Book Academy (CBA) to gather a prayer team to lean on for accountability and, most importantly, prayer. These people have been praying through my ups and downs in this process, and I am forever grateful to them. Thank you to Kathy Alred, June Murray, Keri Jacquemain, Deanna Joseph, Lisa and Fred Hartman, and to my dear husband, David Cruickshank.

Through CBA, CJ and Shelley Hitz focus on training writers and authors to write and self-publish from a Christian perspective. They have provided invaluable education, resources, and guidance. Thanks to you both, along with the CBA team and my fellow "authors in progress."

A special thank you to my fantastic editor, Katie Erickson, for her unique expertise, guidance, and support.

My personal group of supporters recently grew with an additional member, Kathryn Wright, who agreed to be a beta reader, along with Kathy Alred. Although the two Kathys don't know each other personally, they are both faith-filled women who love the Lord and are witnesses to the gospel in their own unique ways. Thank you!

Contents

Chapter One: Something's Wrong

When the phone rang that evening, I never thought I'd hear the words, "You've already had a heart attack. You failed your stress test today."

"What? Are you sure," I asked, stunned. "Yes," the cardiologist said, "I'm sure. Come to the hospital in the morning for a cardiac catheterization."

I knew for a long time that something was wrong. I mean a long time. My life was very busy with work and graduate school. I was pushing my mental and emotional limits to the extreme. And now my body was reacting to the stress physically. It made sense that eventually something was going to "give." I just wasn't ready for it now.

I was too busy to slow down, to lighten up on the reins of my life. There was just too much at stake. Frankly, both my job and my graduate school studies were on the line if I had to take time off from either.

"How did I get in this position," I asked myself. I felt trapped and out of control, like someone chained to a treadmill that never stopped moving. This feeling had not come about quickly. Slowly, but steadily, it grew as I realized (very late in the process) that my enthusiasm for work, for helping people, had collided with a definite tendency toward perfectionism. As compassionate and caring as I was towards the clients I served, I was ultimately doing a disservice to my own mental and physical health.

Work

My career began with all the best intentions. In fact, I *still* believe helping people is my ultimate purpose in life. It's the balance between personal and professional life where my struggle has been. Perhaps you may relate to this: to be caught between two priorities, both of high value and meaning.

My professional mental health career began in rural southeastern North Carolina in 1980, working as the coordinator for a Sheltered Workshop Program, also referred to as a Community Living Skills (CLS) program. I coordinated this program for adults with severe and profound developmental disabilities, as well as supervised the staff members who provided services to these clients.

After a short time, I was promoted to a larger Sheltered Workshop Program, known as an Adult Developmental Activities Program (ADAP), coordinating services for adults with moderate to mild developmental disabilities, along with supervising staff members who provided firsthand services for these individuals.

These two positions came about due to my experience with adults who had a full range of developmental disabilities, fragile medical conditions, and psychiatric disorders during a six-month internship in Michigan, following my Bachelor of Music degree in Music Therapy. I was in my early twenties, energetic, and ready to help people.

Even though I enjoyed advocating and vocationally equipping people with developmental disabilities, my greater interest was helping people with mental illnesses. When a position as a Social Worker opened up in 1984 within the same county mental health system, I applied, interviewed, and secured the position. I worked as a therapist and later as a supervisor from 1984 until 2003. It was this move into the

Social Work field that began my true mental health focus and career until retiring thirty-eight years later.

A proponent of education and learning in general, I had always wanted to pursue a master's degree. There weren't any Master of Social Work (MSW) degrees available in my area during the early years of my social work career. Thus, I studied for and earned a Master of Education in Educational Administration at a local university, which at the time was a branch of the University of North Carolina. That experience whet my appetite for more graduate-level education.

School

While employed as a Social Worker III, I had the unique opportunity to pursue an MSW degree. You may wonder how someone with a Bachelor of Music Therapy degree would come to work as a Social Worker in a large, rural community mental health center. Let me explain.

During the 1980s and 1990s in North Carolina, a Social Work degree was not required to work in a Social Work position. I grandfathered into this field through continuing education, experience, and licensure testing.

Even as a licensed Social Worker, there was a possibility this grandfathering clause could be removed in the future. I needed and wanted to obtain an MSW degree.

I applied to a special MSW program through East Carolina University (ECU) and Pembroke State University (now known as the University of North Carolina at Pembroke). It was at UNCP that I previously earned a Master of Education degree. I was accepted into this special cohort-based MSW program.

The program was designed as a three-year, part-time program. In order to participate, however, students had to attend classes several nights a week and on Saturdays. Saturday classes were at ECU, which is about a three-hour drive one way from home. In addition, several practicum placements and completion of a thesis was required. Oh, and did I forget to mention that I worked full time these three years as well?

During the first few years, before my schedule became too grueling, I also worked part-time in the UNCP Music Department as a woodwind instructor. In total, I taught woodwinds at the university for 14 years. I was also involved in other musical activities, such as performing in faculty recitals, various university pit orchestras, adjudicating Solo & Ensemble competitions, performing with several regional theater orchestras, a regional concert band, the Fayetteville Symphony Orchestra for a season, and leading my church's music ministry.

When required to travel back and forth to ECU, I couldn't continue with my musical commitments, other than leading the music ministry at church. My focus had to be on work and school.

Evening classes were held in Fayetteville, NC, about 35 miles from home. Some of the classes were taught at a local AHEC (area health education) program. Others were taught at Fort Bragg and/or Pope Air Force Base. It was quite the experience!

Practicums were both interesting and varied. Most enjoyable was working with my mental health center's substance abuse department. There, my role was conducting intakes and assigning clients to the treatment programs that were available, both in-patient and out-patient. My supervisor was inspiring; a lively, ambitious person, full of both common sense and street smarts. I appreciated her encouragement. She knew I enjoyed this position, but she also knew that I had little experience in this field. I was eager to take on this challenge.

The work had to be fast, but thorough. I learned much about interviewing techniques and being quick on my feet. The job took knowledge, an ability to relate to others therapeutically, discernment, and intuitiveness. Decisions about the course of treatment had to be made by the time the intake was concluded. Treatment is time-sensitive in the substance abuse world. I learned an incredible amount about substances, abuse/addiction, and human nature while in that practicum. It was one of the most enjoyable roles of my career!

This particular practicum placement was a job-swap agreement with our mental health administrator between me and a fellow Social Worker/ECU student who worked in the same facility as mine. I took on a substance abuse intake position while the other student took on my caseload of clients. In this situation, the agreement was that if either one of us could not fulfill our designated job-swap duties, the practicum placement ended. We only had one chance to make this special agreement work, so, to say the least, the pressure was on.

My normal (full-time) Social Work position was demanding in and of itself. Caseload sizes went as high as 165 clients. During graduate school, my caseload was approximately 120 clients, but they were more complicated in nature – for example, dual diagnosis clients and high profile, complex cases.

The Problem

Don't get me wrong, I loved the challenge of school and work, and I learned a tremendous amount during this time. But there was a physical and emotional toll. The stress was unrelenting. I was overwhelmed and often felt as if I didn't know what the next right thing was. I did not take good care of myself (I lived alone), and my sleep suffered tremendously. I was anxious and overstimulated by anything that wasn't related to work or study. I vividly remember waking up several times at two o'clock in the morning, suddenly realizing I had a paper due that same day. In my life, most of my papers were written in their final draft form the first time around. Rough drafts were a thing of dreams. Every day, I just did the best that I could do.

Several times a year, my parents would visit and stay for about a week. They were an absolute blessing to me, helping do things around the house that were otherwise neglected. Dad did house maintenance and repairs. He also took my dog out for long walks, happily becoming walking buddies during their stays. Mom would sometimes drive me to ECU because I had become agoraphobic and feared driving long distances. She would spend time in the library looking for resources for me on anxiety and crisis theory, which ironically was my thesis topic, while I was in class.

Eventually, however, despite my family's ongoing emotional support and my efforts to cope, it was too hard to maintain my pace with my level of stress.

Chapter Two: Circling the Wagons

When you are young, new to your profession, and are challenged by what you do, your energy can feel endless. Can you relate to this? Have you ever had a new job or perhaps an exciting project and wanted to focus solely on that? Perhaps you are fueled with an eagerness and enthusiasm, as well as a desire to make a mark in the world. In my case, I wanted to help people. I wanted to learn as much as possible to be able to treat people with difficult, complex psychological problems. I loved the field of mental health. Anything concerning feelings, behavior, or the mind was intriguing. I still feel strongly about this – both an interest in mental health as well as the desire to learn and grow, although my areas of interest in learning new things have become more extensive with age. By the way, I consider this a good thing!

When I began my professional career, I jumped in with both feet, priding myself on giving my clients one hundred percent of my attention, sometimes even more than one hundred percent. I am still proud of this; however, there's the realization that giving this kind of effort continuously over the years can lead to an imbalanced life. One in which clients get more of you than you give to yourself.

Over time, this leads to damage physically and emotionally, and eventually, has the potential to negatively impact the people I was striving to help. At the time, however, in my naivete, I didn't realize this. I think that if I had, I still wouldn't have changed much, due to my idealism and stubbornness, having an internal philosophy of "I can do it."

I remember a professor in graduate school who reminded us that we couldn't "fix" anybody. I didn't want to believe her – although she was correct.

Gradually, my strength and energy began to wane, while continuing to work 100+ percent with my clients. I started feeling more anxious, worried that perhaps I *was* trying to do too much. To my detriment, I ended up using that anxiety to propel myself deeper into an emotional and physical chasm. So, there I was, feeling anxious due to self-imposed stress. But, instead of heeding that anxiety, I used it to push myself even harder.

I continued to tell myself I was doing the right thing by helping others. I forgot that I needed to help myself, too.

Love Your Neighbor

While attending church growing up, I remember hearing the Scripture verse from Matthew 22, when a Pharisee tried to trap Jesus with this question:

> *"Teacher, which is the most important commandment in the law of Moses?" Jesus replied, 'You must love the Lord your God with all your heart, all your soul, and all your mind.' This is the first and greatest commandment. A second is equally important: 'Love your neighbor as yourself.' The entire law and all the demands of the prophets are based on these two commandments."*
> *(Matthew 22:36-40 NLT)*

Honestly, it wasn't until just a few years ago that I even acknowledged the *"yourself"* part of *"Love your neighbor as yourself."* I never focused on the "me" part, only the "neighbor part."

While busy with workaholic blinders on, I became very proficient at loving my "neighbors": my clients, my family, my friends. Slowly but surely, anxiety turned into despair and anger, as my level of energy and enthusiasm fizzled. Mind you, this was a slow, insidious journey. A process that, for much of the time, was going down a road of denial. Every once in a while, I looked up from my path and saw life as it really was. I saw that not only was my emotional self falling apart, but so was my body. I wasn't listening to or heeding Jesus' commandment, *"Love your neighbor as yourself."*

Anxiety and stress can be felt in many parts of our bodies. We can experience headaches, stomachaches, and illnesses of our immune system. For me, it seemed like these symptoms hopped around from one body system to another, in an effort to get my attention. These symptoms and ailments were red flags telling me to slow down, to stop, to readjust. But if the pain wasn't bad enough to stop me, I'd continue plodding down my own path of self-destruction in the name of altruism. That is until I could no longer ignore my body's signals for help.

I began to experience migraine headaches that were serious enough that my neurologist ordered an emergency CT scan of my brain. At one point I had a migraine headache that lasted 15 days straight.

Anxiety and Heartache

What *got* my attention was when the pain moved to my chest. This was a pain of enough severity and length of time that I could no longer ignore my body's distress signals. It was time to circle the wagons.

I was worried. Really worried. In my mind, I knew that chest pains were not to be ignored. It's not the type of pain that you can deny or put off, at least not for long. This situation was becoming more and more serious. I was worried about what was happening, worried about the future, pretty much worried about everything. I was fearful to go to work, fearful of going to school. And yet I continued to do both.

I had weekly long-distance phone calls with my parents during this time (when long-distance phone calls were expensive)! For a long time, I probably minimized my concerns in an effort to prove my ability to work hard and be independent. My mistake in this, however, was that I didn't have an accurate idea in my mind about how much work was too much work. I admit my penchant for perfectionism and a desire to please others!

Over time, however, my parents could tell that something was wrong and that a visit for more than a week or two to North Carolina may be necessary. So, here's the plan that was devised through the support of my parents, who knew I was probably having difficulty making good personal decisions at this point.

I made an appointment with a cardiologist, who began to treat me. In the meantime, my parents decided to travel to North Carolina to stay until my situation was resolved. I later learned that they had contacted a realtor in the area to look at the possibility of moving to North Carolina to help me, in case I could not manage living on my own.

The Stress Test

My parents arrived shortly before I was scheduled for a Persantine Stress Test. This is the kind of stress test where you don't walk on the treadmill but rather lie on a table while a radioactive substance is injected into your body to mimic the speeding up and racing of your heart (a.k.a. "stress").

By this time in my journey, my anxiety was very high, and I had begun to experience panic attacks. I had entered counseling several weeks earlier. The counselor suggested a variety of meditation and breathing techniques. But perhaps even more importantly, she was a trained expert in biofeedback, and she shared these techniques with me. I was a good fit for this therapeutic intervention and was able to use it effectively, first with her biofeedback equipment and then later on my own.

I am indebted to her for providing me with my personal anxiety-reducing techniques, which were helpful then and are still useful today.

Despite these techniques, however, the anxiety and chest pain were getting the best of me.

The panic attacks seemed to be coming on me in waves, especially on the day of the Persantine Stress Test. That was a rough day. A day of anxiety, pain, and uncertainty. My energy level was so low, I remember I had to have help getting dressed after the procedure. But even that doesn't adequately describe how I felt.

I was shaky and weak. It was like I was moving on autopilot, merely going through the motions. Other people had to make the most minor decisions for me. “It’s time to get your clothes on. Maybe you should use the restroom.” It was as if I was no longer there in the room, which I thought was fine. I had no desire to be there anyway. I couldn’t think about it. Nor did I want to. I just wanted this feeling to be over.

Gradually, ever so gradually, I began to “come back” into the room at the hospital after being evaluated. I was tired, oh so tired. Still not knowing what to think. Wondering what was next. Grateful beyond words that my parents were there. I needed to be loved at that moment like a child. I needed to be free of responsibility for just a little while. To rest. To be. To be free of the confinement of the stress that I had imprisoned myself with for too long.

And then, that same evening, the phone rang.

Chapter Three: A Clean Heart, God?

It was almost impossible to process the words the doctor said on the phone. "You've already had a heart attack. You failed your stress test today. Come to the hospital in the morning for a cardiac catheterization." "It must be true," I thought. "It was the doctor himself who called. It must be serious." Still, I didn't really believe it. It felt as if I was trapped in a dream. It was too much to process. Just too much.

I didn't think or speak much about the situation with my family after the call. What could I say? I had no more words for something that I felt deep in my heart was untrue.

My anxiety seemed to suddenly abate, only to be replaced with emotional numbness. So, I went into autopilot mode again. I knew how to do that only too well. Stressed? It's OK. Carry on, sister! My solution was that I should go to bed early because I was due at the hospital by 5:30 the next morning.

How do people describe this kind of event? Surreal? “Yes, that’s it,” I thought. “Yes, carry on, no matter the consequences.” I had become a sad, fragile expert in denial. So, I went to bed.

The Night Before My Cardiac Catheterization

In therapy I had learned several meditation and breathing techniques to reduce anxiety. That night I used a Centering technique to help me fall asleep. Centering is a simple technique to explain, yet it takes practice to be effective. Basically, one focuses their mind on the inhale and exhale of their breath. If any thoughts enter during this practice (which, believe me, they will!), all you need to do is refocus your attention on your breath again. The goal I had was to work up to 30 minutes of meditation, beginning with two minutes and then adding minutes incrementally. I was told that 30 minutes of meditation is the equivalent of five hours of sleep.

Fortunately, I was able to concentrate on my breath going in and out of my body and to gently push aside any thoughts that entered my mind that distracted me from my focus. Slowly, I felt myself relax and the darkness behind my closed eyes became even darker. I could feel myself sinking into a place of comfort and safety. I drifted off to sleep.

Surprisingly, I slept well. It was as if my mind was able to let go of my worries for those precious hours of rest. Thank You, Lord.

Music in the Morning

I awoke in the morning with music in my ears, echoing the tune of a psalm I remember singing in church services as a child and a young adult, *"Create in me a clean heart, O God."* Was it God that placed this psalm in my mind and on my heart? I wanted to believe that it was, because accompanying what I heard was a feeling of amazing peace.

"Create in me a clean heart, O God;
and renew a right spirit within me.
Cast me not away from thy presence;
and take not thy holy spirit from me.
Restore unto me the joy of thy salvation;
and uphold me with thy free spirit."
(Psalm 51:10-12 KJV)

A clean heart, God? I desperately prayed for this to be true. I prayed He would be with me today, no matter what the outcome. God is in control, not me. This day, and every day, is truly His. I didn't know how my life would change after the cardiac catheterization. But I had to trust Him. So, I did.

The Power of Breathing

My parents and I arrived at the hospital as scheduled, and I prepared for the cardiac catheterization. There were questions to answer, papers to sign, clothes to change, and IVs to be inserted.

This is where I should probably mention that I am very fearful of IVs. Needles and I don't get along with each other. During the IV insertion process, the nurses became acutely aware of this anxiety. A new plan of action was developed. Before the catheterization, I was to receive Valium through the IV to help with relaxation and calming.

While waiting in the pre-op area, I began a breathing exercise as another way to reduce anxiety. It has been called 4-8 Breathing, a very simple yet effective technique. You inhale through your nose for a count of four and then exhale through your mouth with a slow count of eight. What makes 4-8 Breathing great is that it is fairly unobtrusive. You can practically do it anywhere without being noticed, especially if you do it quietly. Also, there's no set duration for 4-8 Breathing. You can continue the process as long as you wish.

I began my 4-8 Breathing, and a good amount of time passed by. The nurse stepped in and out of the room occasionally to check on me. I was feeling really relaxed and ready for the procedure.

Later, the nurse came in and told me she was there to give me the Valium injection through the IV. Honestly, I thought it had already been given to me – I was that relaxed!

Our bodies are truly amazing, especially with what they can do to help us in times of pain, or anxiety, or distress. For example, look at the healing and restorative properties of our breath, which is God given. I will never underestimate the power of the breath in my lungs and remember who gave me this breath of life.

It was now time to enter the operating room to have the procedure.

Ballet of the Heart

I was surprised by the activity in the room. Everywhere I looked, I saw colorful monitors, some with vital signs displayed and some that looked like TV monitors. People were moving around quickly, each one intent on their tasks. I was to be awake during the procedure, which I didn't care for. But I wasn't given a choice. Oh well. Carry on,

I was sedated to the point that it seemed like I was a member of the audience looking on stage at a medical ballet, watching bright lights, precise movements, and hearing a cacophony of beeps, blips, and chatter. A dance of life, if you will.

The doctor invited me to watch the catheter traveling through my femoral artery to my heart on one of the TV monitors, but I declined. No, I was content just looking around at all the dancers and listening to the soundtrack of the show.

I don't remember how long I was in that room that had seen so many life and death situations over the years. After a while, I sort of detached from the reality of it all, and time went on. Feeling fairly calm by this point, I just gave into the hands of the doctor and God. A peaceful surrender.

Then the doctor spoke to me, telling me he wanted to give me the results of the procedure while I was still in the operating room. "While I'm still on the table?" My God.

Chapter Four: Getting to the Heart of the Matter

"Why would the doctor want to talk to me while I was still in the operating room," I wondered. I feared that there was a problem with my heart after all, and that I needed immediate surgery of some kind. Right then and there. This really couldn't be happening. Could it?

I remember seeing the doctor bend over the operating room table to look in my eyes. He didn't look upset or even concerned. Instead, he was smiling. I felt suspended in time for those brief moments before he spoke.

Then he said that my heart was fine. Fine. "Did you hear that, Lord?" Of course He did. He already knew. Relief, thankfulness, and gratefulness flooded through my body.

There were no blockages anywhere in my heart and no evidence of a previous heart attack. Later, I learned there had been an error in the stress test I had the day before. An error. No heart problems.

Deep down, I knew this was true. I never fully believed my heart was faulty. I felt certain I would have known if I had ever had a heart attack. Some people have silent heart attacks, but there was something inside of me that was convinced otherwise.

There were so many gentle hints and notes from God that everything would be well with my heart. He even woke me up earlier that morning with *"Create in me a clean heart, O God"* playing in my soul. God is good, friends!

My Second Chance

I realized God had given me a second chance. My heart was healthy, and a major crisis had been averted. What an incredible gift! I didn't earn this. I didn't deserve it. Yet, He loved me enough then (and now) to walk with me through fear and pain and uncertainty.

Not only was this a gift, but it was a lesson that will remain with me for the rest of my life. God taught me life is precious and should not be taken for granted. He wants to be in relationship with me, and with you too. His love for us cannot be measured.

I knew I would still have to face many obstacles and challenges with my anxious thinking and behavior. My stress levels were still too high. Change was needed. And balance. Real balance in my life. Not to just try to find an easier and faster way to run on the work and school treadmill like a hamster going nowhere fast.

God gave me a second chance to reflect on my life and the decisions from the past. A second chance to change things now and in the future. It would be up to me to decide to change both my mindset and my behaviors.

Indeed, I needed to make positive changes in order to have a more peaceful life. To have a life, learning to really love my neighbors as I love myself, instead of giving all my energy to only others. To have more balance, rest, and a sense of true purpose.

And most importantly, a second chance to grow closer to God in what I think, believe, and do.

Lessons Learned

This is my second-chance story. There have been many second chances in my life, but the memory of this experience has remained with me for decades. I never want to forget it. In fact, I pray that I can still learn from it today.

As I write this testimony, many years have passed. I have grown and changed. I am far from perfect, but I can say with confidence that I understand more.

Most importantly, my faith in God, Jesus Christ, and the Holy Spirit has grown. I remain excited to learn as much as I can about being in relationship with God, Three in One.

Recently, I read a verse from Exodus that resonated deeply with me. It seemed absolutely perfect that this verse came to my awareness while writing this book. It summarizes my second chance experience with God simply, yet profoundly.

The words are part of a song known as the Song of Moses and Miriam. It was written to celebrate the victory of the Israelites fleeing Egypt when God parted the Red Sea. God rescued His people, leading them to safety, and the people celebrated by singing:

"The Lord is my strength and my song."
(Exodus 15:2 NLT)

The Lord is my strength and song, too. He gives me strength when I am weak. And He is my song. I will praise Him forever!

Invitation

Do you have a second-chance story? I believe we all have stories to share where God has shown His grace and mercy in our lives.

He loves us and wants us to be with Him. We are His children, and He is our Heavenly Father. He is ready, willing, and able to give us second chances. And third chances. And many more chances after that. His love for us is limitless, as is His desire for us to seek Him out every day of our lives.

Being given a second chance from God doesn't mean that you will take it. Don't get me wrong, I pray that you do. But taking a second chance means taking action in our lives. It's not just deciding to change, or stating a desire for change to others. We need to actually change.

We need to turn away from something negative in our lives or turn toward something positive. Sometimes we need to do both. And then we need to remain constant not only in our commitment to that change, but consistent with the actions required to have that change happen.

And that is not an easy thing to do, especially if our second chance from God is a really big chance.

You'll know what you need to do. And if you don't, or if you're unsure about your next steps, pray. Or talk to someone whom you trust has your best interests at heart. Or do both. Journal your thoughts, feelings, and questions. Then take your journaling time to God in prayer. Search your heart. God will be cheering you on. Remember, He wants you to come to Him. You are precious to Him.

If you see a glimmer of a second chance in your life now, today, I encourage you to take it. God is reaching out to you, no matter how difficult your life has been so far. Reach out. Clasp His hand. He will never let go of you. If anyone does let go, it will be you moving away from Him. Don't let that happen, please.

I promise you that it will always be worth it to take the second chances that God offers. He will never lead you astray. Listen for that gentle whisper in your soul, that careful nudge that draws you forward. And if you are ever in doubt about whether or not you should move one way or another, know that God will never guide you in any way, shape, or form, that is contrary to His

Holy Word, the Bible. He is the same God yesterday, today, and forever.

So, take heart, my friend. Listen and look for the presence of God in your life. He is in all things. And sometimes, perhaps when you least expect it, He will show up and pave the way for you to have a more peaceful, strengthened, and joyous life through His offer of a second chance. Take Him up on His offer.

Note from the Author

Reviews are priceless to authors! If you have enjoyed this book, would you consider reviewing it on Amazon.com? Find the book and then click Write a Review. Thank you!

Bonus for You

Journaling is an excellent way to process our thoughts and feelings, especially when we feel we need to make changes in our lives. When God gives us second chances, He is offering us an amazing gift. But it is up to us how we use these gifts. Writing down our thoughts and questions can help us to listen for God's guiding words to put those second chances into action.

I have a gift of 120 prompts and questions for you to download, to help you determine where you currently are in life and where you want to be in your future. Remember, with God's help, anything is possible. Download this bonus at:

www.jeaninemjonesauthor.com.

About the Author

Jeanine M. Jones is a retired Clinical Social Worker, with thirty-eight years of experience in the mental health field, having worked in North Carolina and Michigan.

Since retiring, Jeanine enjoys writing, playing the clarinet in a local community concert band, and working with the Stephen Ministry program at her church.

She currently lives with her husband in Macomb County, Michigan.